WITHDRAWN

Spotlight on
ANCIENT CIVILIZATIONS
ROME

Ancient Roman
GOVERNMENT

Amelie von Zumbusch

Published in 2014 by The Rosen Publishing Group, Inc.
29 East 21st Street, New York, NY 10010

First Edition

Book Design: Kate Vlachos
Layout Design: Andrew Povolny

Library of Congress Cataloging-in-Publication Data

Zumbusch, Amelie von.
  Ancient Roman government / by Amelie von Zumbusch. – First edition.
    pages cm. – (Spotlight on ancient civilizations: Rome)
  Includes index.
  ISBN 978-1-4777-0776-0 (library binding) – ISBN 978-1-4777-0885-9 (pbk.) – ISBN 978-1-4777-0886-6 (6-pack)
  1. Rome–History–Republic, 265-30 B.C.–Juvenile literature. 2. Rome–Politics and government–265-30 B.C.–Juvenile literature. 3. Rome–History–Republic, 265-30 B.C.–Comic books, strips, etc. 4. Rome–Politics and government–265-30 B.C.–Comic books, strips, etc. 5. Graphic novels. I. Title.
  DG254.Z86 2014
  937–dc23
                                        2012051006

Manufactured in the United States of America

CPSIA Compliance Information: Batch #S13PK2: For Further Information contact Rosen Publishing, New York, New York at 1-800-237-9932

CONTENTS

Change over Time

Ancient Rome was a powerful **civilization** that lasted for over a thousand years. During its history, Roman civilization changed in many ways. Some of the biggest changes were in its government.

This statue is of Rome's fourth emperor, Claudius. He ruled from AD 41 to 54.

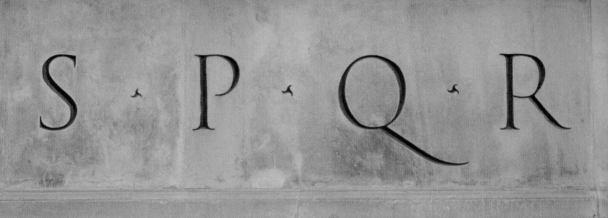

SPQR stands for Senatus Populusque Romanus, which means "the Senate and the people of Rome." It appeared on many things in ancient Roman times and is still used today.

In its earliest years, Rome was ruled by kings. Then, the kings were overthrown and the Roman Republic was founded. During the republic, power was spread around. There were many **magistrates**, or **elected** officials. Groups with many members, such as the Senate and Plebeian Assembly, were important. Rome's first **emperor**, Augustus, took power in 27 BC. He and the long string of emperors that followed ruled the Roman Empire.

Founding Rome

The Romans believed that Rome's founder and first king was named Romulus. In their stories, Romulus and his twin brother, Remus, were the grandsons of the king of Alba Longa, a city near Rome. As babies, they were cared for by a wolf after being left to die. As adults, they decided to found a city. Romulus killed Remus in a fight over the city they were building.

In Roman stories, Romulus and Remus are the sons of Mars (left) and Rhea Silvia (right). Mars was the god of war. Rhea Silvia's father was the king of Alba Longa.

The story of Romulus and Remus was important to the Romans. This image of the wolf that raised them comes from a Roman settlement in Great Britain.

Historians doubt this story is true. However, they think a people called the Latins who came from Alba Longa did settle Rome. These early settlers fought with and later joined with a neighboring people called the Sabines.

The Kings of Rome

Roman stories tell of seven kings who ruled Rome between 753 and 509 BC. One of the kings was Numa Pompilius, who established many Roman religious **customs**. Another was Tullus Hostilius, who **conquered** Alba Longa.

Though its power varied over time, the Roman Senate lasted for basically all of Rome's history. This carving shows senators, or members of the Senate.

These wall paintings are from an Etruscan tomb. Though the Romans fought several wars against the Etruscans, they also borrowed many things from Etruscan culture.

Historians doubt that the list of kings is accurate. However, they think the early Romans did elect kings to lead them. Once elected, the kings had total power. If they wanted advice, they would consult with a group of elders, called the Senate.

Several of Rome's later kings were Etruscan. The Etruscans were a neighboring people. Rome's Etruscan kings undertook many building projects and introduced Etruscan **culture** to Rome.

Setting Up the Republic

Stories say that Rome's last king, Tarquinius Superbus, misused his powers. This **inspired** the people of Rome to overthrow him and set up a new government. Rome became a republic. Instead of having a king, it was ruled by two consuls. They served for just one year. The popular assemblies elected consuls. Assemblies were made up of groups of Roman citizens. Other magistrates, such as praetors, had power, too.

Though the Senate had existed under the kings, its power grew during the Roman Republic. For example, it controlled spending. It was made up of **patricians**, or members of the oldest families.

This statue is thought to be of Lucius Junius Brutus. He helped found the Roman Republic and was one of the first consuls.

Patricians and Plebeians

The patricians had most of the power in the early republic. However, most Roman citizens were plebeians. Plebeians included farmers, shopkeepers, craftspeople, and more. They were usually poorer than patricians.

This carving shows a Roman blacksmith and his tools. Blacksmiths make things out of metal. Roman craftspeople, such as blacksmiths, were mostly plebeians.

Patricians were better represented in Rome's assemblies than the plebeians were. Plebeians were not allowed to be consuls or senators. Until 445 BC, it was against the law for plebeians to marry patricians.

The plebeians kept fighting for equal rights. In 494 BC, they withdrew from the city and formed their own assembly.

They came back after the patricians agreed to add officials, called tribunes and aediles, to represent the plebeians.

Family history was very important to Roman patricians. This statue shows a Roman patrician holding busts of family members who had died.

The Plebeians' Power Grows

The plebeians withdrew from Rome several times over the next few hundred years to protest their unfair treatment. Around 450 BC, they got the patricians to agree to write down Rome's rules. This code became known as the Law of the Twelve Tables. In 367 BC, plebeians won the right to be elected consul.

In time, the plebeians won the right to hold other positions, such as that of **censor**. In 287 BC, the patricians agreed that laws passed by the Plebeian Assembly would apply to all Romans. However, old, rich families continued to play a big role in government.

This carving shows a Roman censor at a religious ceremony. Censors maintained public morals. They also directed the census, or count of Roman citizens.

Wars Pull the Republic Apart

While the plebeians and patricians struggled for control of Rome's government, Rome's power was growing. The Romans conquered other peoples, first in Italy and later in Asia, Africa, and other parts of Europe. Rome was often at war. The wars led to problems in Roman society. This included a big gap between the rich and the poor. Wars broke out among Roman leaders.

Julius Caesar was a very successful general. He conquered much of Europe for Rome.

General Julius Caesar emerged as the winner of these wars in the 40s BC. In 44, he was named **dictator**, or sole ruler, for life. The Romans had elected dictators during past emergencies. However, these dictators originally served for just six months.

This carving shows a Roman soldier and centurion, or military officer. Rome's army was made up of units called legions. Every person in a legion had an exact job.

From Republic to Empire

Julius Caesar was killed in 44 BC. By then, the Roman Republic was falling apart. Roman leaders continued to fight for control. By 31 BC, Julius Caesar's great-nephew, Octavian, became Rome's leader. In 27 BC, he took the name Augustus and became Rome's first emperor.

Octavian defeated his opponents for good in the Battle of Actium. This carving shows his triumph, which was an event held in honor of his win.

Augustus lived in a house on Rome's Palatine Hill. This painted room is one of several in the house that people can visit today.

This Roman coin has a picture of Augustus Caesar on it.

The Senate continued to meet under Augustus. However, the emperor had the real power. Since Romans still did not like the idea of kings, he was known as the *princeps,* or "first." Augustus set many **reforms** in place. He changed how the **provinces** controlled by Rome were ruled. He backed major building projects, too.

Rome's Emperors

When Augustus died in AD 14, his stepson Tiberius became Rome's next emperor. In all, five members of Augustus's family would go on to be emperors. Some helped Rome grow. Others terrorized the people of Rome with their great power. The emperor Nero even had his own mother killed!

Tiberius served as emperor from AD 14 to 37.

This carving shows an emperor giving out money to the Roman people. The carving is part of the Arch of Constantine, in Rome.

Even after Augustus's family died out, Rome continued to be ruled by emperors. Some, such as Marcus Aurelius, are remembered as wise rulers. Others are remembered for their crazy or violent behavior. Though emperors were hugely powerful, they risked being killed if they lost the army's backing or made too many enemies.

Leaders Look to Rome

People are still fascinated by ancient Rome. Many are dazzled by stories of the rich and powerful emperors. The stages Rome's government went through also help us understand how civilizations change over time. For example, you can see how Rome's early kings helped shape its later history.

The founders of the United States were inspired by the Roman Republic. They agreed that distributing power to many people was a good idea. They also embraced the Roman idea that every citizen deserves equal treatment before the law.

Rome's Senate and public assemblies were important models for the US Congress.

GLOSSARY

censor (SEN-ser) A Roman official in charge of officially counting people and maintaining public morals.

civilization (sih-vih-lih-ZAY-shun) People living in a certain way.

conquered (KON-kerd) Overcame.

culture (KUL-chur) The beliefs, practices, and arts of a group of people.

customs (KUS-tums) Practices common to many people in a place or a social class.

dictator (DIK-tay-ter) A person who takes power and has total control over others.

elected (ee-LEK-tid) Picked for an office by voters.

emperor (EM-per-er) The ruler of an empire or of several countries.

inspired (in-SPY-urd) Moved someone to do something.

magistrates (MA-jih-strayts) Officials who make sure that laws are obeyed.

patricians (puh-TRI-shunz) Members of the oldest, most powerful families.

provinces (PRAH-vin-sez) Lands that are run by another country.

reforms (rih-FORMZ) Changes or improvements.

INDEX

WEBSITES

Due to the changing nature of Internet links, PowerKids Press has developed an online list of websites related to the subject of this book. This site is updated regularly. Please use this link to access the list: www.powerkidslinks.com/sacr/gov/